How to Attract Your Twin Flame Quickly and Easily

Liliah Raye

Copyright © 2020

All Rights Reserved. No part of this publication may be reproduced, stored in a retrieval system or transmitted, in any form or by any means, electronic, mechanical, photocopying, recording or otherwise, without the written permission of the copyright holder.

~

To all of my beautiful readers

~

Introduction

Have you ever heard of the term *twin flames*? Twin flames are 2 souls who were originally 1 soul. At some point, that 1 soul was split into 2. When twin flames unite, they connect so deeply that they feel like 1 person.

In a twin flame relationship, there is a lot of love, respect, consideration, depth and spiritual growth happening. Twin flames are so happy together that they help other people be happy too. In fact, when twin flames unite on Earth, they raise the vibration of the whole planet. These are the reasons why so many persons want to find their twin flames.

Many people talk about finding *the one* for them. Do you know what *the one* means? When someone is looking for the one for them, they're really looking for their twin flame. Your twin flame is the one for you, and you deserve to be with them. Sadly, countless women and men are not with their twin flames. Numerous persons are looking for their twin flames but are not finding them. Some are preventing themselves from meeting their twin flames by having mental blocks against being in relationships. Others choose to stay with bad people who hurt them or don't care enough. These suffer in toxic and low-quality relationships but don't want to leave.

There is no reason to stay in a relationship that is not romantically fulfilling. You shouldn't let any selfish bastard guilt you into staying with them by telling you how much they've done for you. No matter how much a person has helped you, you do not owe them your heart or body. You don't owe *anyone* your heart or body, even if you're married to them. Also, don't fall for the *getting divorced is a sin* nonsense. Staying in an unhappy marriage is what would be sinful. To sin is to act in way that brings physical, mental or emotional harm to yourself or another person. If you're in an unhappy marriage, feel free to cancel any vows that you've made, and move on.

I must ask you, are you someone who's willing to settle for just about anyone who'd have you? Do you want to continue trying or putting up with someone who isn't pulling their weight in the relationship? Or, do you want a fantastic and fulfilling relationship? If you want a fantastic and fulfilling relationship, then you'd need to be united with your twin flame. In this book, I will show you how to easily attract your twin flame – and fast.

The 7-step formula given here in this book is what I used to call in my twin flame. When I completed the 7 steps of this formula, she came into my life like lightning.

It's Okay if you don't believe in twin flames. If you want to attract a romantic partner who'll help you have the greatest happiness and peace, this book will help you call them in, easily and quickly.

Signs of a Twin Flame Relationship

A twin flame relationship is very different from other kinds of relationships. When it comes to romantic relationships, twin flame unions are the best. Twin flame couples are the happiest in their romantic partnerships and marriages. Before I give the 7-step twin flame union formula, here are the signs of a twin flame relationship.

Twin flames:

- ✓ Trust each other
- ✓ Love each other deeply and unconditionally
- ✓ Are considerate to each other
- ✓ Prioritize each other
- ✓ Are honest with each other
- ✓ Connect on all levels: spiritually, mentally, emotionally and sexually
- ✓ Help each other feel peaceful (there's no "drama" in the relationship)
- ✓ Help each other feel more happy
- ✓ Know the complex and hidden parts of each other

- ✓ Often have the same thoughts or feelings at the same time (even when they're apart)
- ✓ Feel It's safe to be themselves around each other
- ✓ Always enjoy each other's companies
- ✓ Share many of the same interests
- ✓ Find each other beautiful inside and outside
- ✓ Feel a strong desire to touch or be close to each other
- ✓ Do not feel unsure about their relationship
- ✓ Help each other grow spiritually
- ✓ Willingly work out any issues in the relationship

The Twin Flame Union Formula that Works Fast

Did you know that your twin flame is looking for you too? They certainly are. The reason I wrote this book is to help you to connect with them as quickly as possible. I truly believe that The Twin Flame Union Formula will help you find them fast. This formula is made up of 7 steps. I will now list and discuss these steps, and share some of my personal experiences too.

Step One
Love Yourself

Loving yourself is the first and most important thing to do to call in your twin flame. If you don't love yourself, you would prevent your twin flame (as well as other good persons) from coming into your life. People who don't love themselves attract low-vibrational and toxic persons.

Many years ago, I really believed that there were many good persons out there – many good fish in the sea. I used to try to encourage others by telling them this too. Anyway, I learned the hard way that only a small percentage of people in this world are actually *good*. I, like many others, experienced being lied to, mistreated, ghosted by immature and inconsiderate people, and strung along by selfish persons who didn't know what they wanted. I was also sexually taken advantage of by a woman I dated.

Before meeting my twin flame in the middle of 2019, I had never been in a relationship that was mature and fulfilling, but I knew very clearly that I desired a relationship like that. I really wanted a very deep and meaningful connection with someone.

For a long time, I'd been wondering why I was so unlucky in love, and in late 2018, while I was reading something on self-worth, I realized what the main problem was. I realized that I did not love myself enough. Because I didn't really love myself, I was attracting emotionally unavailable and immature persons who couldn't really love anyone.

I was so fed up with these kinds of people coming into my life that I decided to truly love myself. And this is how I did it. **I (1) counted my good qualities, (2) saw myself as a catch, and (3) believed that I deserved someone amazing.** After I did these things, I felt like a new person. I was swimming in positivity and confidence, and I noticed that I started to attract much better persons into my life.

Before I began loving myself, I thought that I could have attracted someone great just by being pretty and agreeable. Boy was I wrong. To my surprise, I wasn't attracting any great romantic prospects. This is because a mature person looking for a relationship would not consider someone who's a people-pleaser or someone who doesn't value themselves much. Do you know the type of individuals that people-pleasers and persons with low self-esteem attract? They attract users, manipulators and narcissists. Trust me – I went through it.

If you asked me if I loved myself before late 2018, I would have immediately said *yes*. How silly I was then... Before late 2018, I cried my eyes out because someone ghosted me. I was even waiting for that same person to contact me again. For another one I wanted, I lowered my standards. I was also romantically involved with someone who was hung up over their ex. This other person couldn't stop talking about their ex and I still wanted them. 2 persons I wanted (at 2 separate times) were emotionally unavailable. There was someone who wasn't sure about me and I still wanted to be with them. One person I loved wanted to *test-drive* me first and I was willing to let them. Someone who I was *more than friends* with forgot a day we had planned to meet and I still continued the relationship with them.

Persons who love themselves know that they deserve great partners. They do not settle for less than they deserve and do not take crap from others. They certainly do not put themselves down for anyone's pleasure or approval. When seeking a relationship, a person who loves themselves wouldn't:

- Consider someone who *throws them breadcrumbs. Breadcrumbing* is leading someone on by contacting them only intermittently to keep them interested.

- Consider someone who feels lukewarm about them
- Date someone who does not forgive
- Entertain an arrogant, narcissistic or selfish person
- Waste a second with someone who's hung up on an ex or anyone else
- Ever contact someone who ghosted them or avoided them
- Lower their standards to please anyone
- Miss an ex who has cheated or ended the relationship

When persons in toxic or abusive relationships start loving themselves, they end it with their partners. If you really love and respect yourself, but your partner/person you're involved with is inconsiderate or isn't really invested, you would naturally and rightly walk out.

If you love yourself, you would hold yourself at a high price. And holding yourself at a high price is how to attract someone of great value.

Step Two
Be Truly Happy

Choose to be genuinely happy. This will really help to call in your twin flame fast. Even though you haven't met the right one as yet, be happy. Even if you're not where you'd like to be at right now, be happy. You might find this won't be easy, but I assure you it is.

The following things will help you be truly happy all the time:

- ✓ Count your blessings every day
- ✓ Appreciate your good qualities, your achievements and how far you've come
- ✓ See the beauty in life
- ✓ Feel a sense of peace believing that good things are going to keep happening to you, and that your life will keep getting better and better

Wise persons understand that happiness doesn't come from other people. Twin flames aren't dependant on each other for happiness, but they do *help* each other have more and more happiness.

Step 3
Be Open-Minded

Before meeting my twin flame Sarah, in 2019, I had a *type*. Before I met her, I wanted a relationship with a lesbian. Before meeting me, Sarah considered herself to be heterosexual. Nevertheless, we were both open-minded. If we weren't, we wouldn't have fallen so deeply in love with each other.

Sarah and I met in a spiritual group. When we started talking, we realized that even though we were from very different backgrounds, we had a lot in common – we even had several phrases/expressions in common. It was very familiar too, like we knew each other from before. We really enjoyed our conversations, and learned from each other. Neither of us was expecting anything. It happened so quickly and so easily that neither of us can recall what the turning point was for us. It came to where I had to ask her if we were official, and she confirmed it. We have no doubt that we are twin flames. After we both agreed that it was official, I spent many days afterwards having to remind myself that I wasn't dreaming – that I was finally with my person.

If you've been imagining your twin flame to look a certain way or have a specific personality, please understand that your twin flame might be *much different* from what you've been imagining. They might be a lot taller or shorter. They might have an unusual accent or voice. They might belong to an ethnic group that you've never considered or be a gender you weren't expecting... Their astrological sign might be one that you don't fancy right now. When you meet your twin flame, it might surprise you, but I assure you that you won't want them to be any different.

Step 4
Feel As If

Feeling as if you already have what you want is a powerful manifestation/attracting technique. To call in your twin flame, practice feeling as if you're already together. Don't visualize anything specific because that would weaken the technique. Just focus on *feeling* as if you're with your twin flame. Feel the exhilaration, satisfaction and appreciation you'd feel as if you're with them. Really immerse yourself in these feelings, and smile if you want. Spend at least a few minutes every day feeling as if you've already met your twin flame.

There is something you can do to make this step even more powerful. You can write a pretend-letter to your twin flame telling them how glad you are to be together. Of course, you won't be sending the letter to anyone. You should keep it somewhere safe like in a drawer or on your computer (if it's digital). Before meeting my twin flame, I wrote a letter to them in 2019. I had no idea who they were going to be… I just wrote them a short but beautiful letter, and in it I told them how happy, right, easy and peaceful everything felt.

Step 5
Find Yourself and Your Path

Your twin flame will come in after you understand yourself and know the path that's right for you. At the time of your meeting, they too will have already found themselves and their path.

When someone has found themselves, they are clear about their likes and dislikes and they understand why they think and respond the way they do. If you're yet in the process of finding yourself, meditation will definitely help you. Mediation has helped me greatly. Simply sitting with a still mind for several minutes is a very powerful meditation practice. If you're having trouble with stilling your mind, it will help to close your eyes and focus on the 3rd eye (the point between your eyebrows). When a thought comes along, just observe it and release it. Keep doing this until your mind is still.

Many people are trying to find the paths that are right for them. **When you're on the path that's right for you, you'll be helping others have true happiness, you'll love what you're doing, and you'll be feeling peace and fulfillment.** If you haven't found your path, all it takes is a little introspection to find out what it is. To find your true path, ask yourself what you enjoy doing most to help others have true happiness.

When you meet your twin flame, both of you will be living in ways that are in agreement with your authentic selves and doing things to help others have true happiness. Both of you would be encouraging and helping each other as well. It shouldn't be surprising if you find that both of you love doing the same things to help people. You might even decide to join forces to help others.

Shortly after we found ourselves and our paths, my twin flame and I met. We were in our mid-thirties when we met. One friend of mine didn't find her twin flame until she was in her 50's. Shortly before meeting her person, she came to the realization of who she was and what her mission was to help humanity.

Sarah and I are both doing things to help others live truly happy lives. I perform energy-healing sessions for others and write spiritual self-help books under my real name. Sarah's work is also spiritual in nature, and helps others live in wisdom, freedom and happiness. We are both honing and expanding our skills so we would be able to help others in more ways.

Step 6
Pray to Spirits of Twin Flame Unions

Spirits of love and light like benevolent angels, gods, goddesses, spirit guides and ascended masters love to help others whenever and in any way they can. It's wise to contact benevolent beings for help in all aspects of life, including help in uniting with your twin flame.

Gods, goddesses, angels, spirit guides and ascended masters who help others in the areas of relationships and marriages can help you to find your twin flame. The following archangels specialize in helping twin flames unite: Chamuel, Raguel, Michael, Jophiel and Raphael. Your own guides, angels and (good) ancestral spirits can help you to find your person too. Find which spirits you feel drawn to and pray to them daily, or as often as you feel appropriate.

The spirits I prayed to for help in finding my twin flame were Archangel Chamuel and my guides.

Step 7
Use Magick

Magick can help persons call in their twin flames quickly and easily. Here I will reveal 5 powerful magickal practices that will help you attract your person. The first 2 are ones I used. Choose one or more of the following to do.

Twin Flame Crystals

The following types of crystals will help to call in your twin flame: Clear Quartz, Rose Quartz, Rhodochrosite, Garnet, Nebula Stone, Rhodonite, Moonstone, Ruby and Twin Crystal (which is a crystal that has 2 terminations at the same end that have developed from the same base). You can use any one of these crystals to help you attract your twin flame. To use a crystal for this purpose, make sure it is cleansed and charged, put your intention into it and then wear it or keep it close to you. You can also wear or place 2 crystals together in your home to attract your twin flame. If you're using 2 crystals, see one as your person and the other as yourself.

It is important to spiritually cleanse and charge your crystals and set your intentions for your crystals before using them. Most crystals need to be occasionally cleansed, charged and have your intentions put into them for them to work effectively.

You can cleanse your crystals by leaving them overnight in the light of the full moon, placing them in running water for about a minute, burying them in salt for about an hour, using Reiki, smudging with white sage, rosemary, peppermint, or palo santo wood for a few minutes, burying them in the earth for twenty-four hours, keeping them with a Selenite or carnelian crystal, chanting a sacred mantra near them 108 times, keeping them with a clear quartz crystal that has been programmed with intention by you or someone else to cleanse other crystals (clear quartz crystals can be programmed for anything), passing them through the flame of a white candle, visualizing them being cleansed with white light for a few minutes, leaving them in sunlight for the day, leaving them out in the rain or playing a singing bowl near to them for a few minutes.

You can charge your crystals by keeping them with a clear quartz crystal that has been programmed to charge other crystals, a piece of Selenite or a Carnelian crystal, leaving them in the light of the full moon for the night, leaving them in sunlight for the day, using Reiki or visualization.

Putting an intention into a crystal is simple. One method is to hold or touch the crystal and say the intention aloud or mentally with faith. To put an intention into your crystal to attract your twin flame, you should hold or touch your crystal/s and mentally or verbally tell it/them to unite you with your twin flame.

You can wear your crystals, carry them in your bag or pocket or place them in your home, car, or office. To attract your twin flame, I highly recommend you wear your twin flame crystal/s or keep them in the relationship corner of your home or room. If you stand in your home with your back facing the front door, the relationship corner is the farthest right hand corner of your home.

Make sure you research your crystals well before using them, so you know their properties and how to take care of them. Some shouldn't be exposed to water because water would cause them to dissolve, crack or rust. Some crystals fade in sunlight and shouldn't be exposed to sunlight.

After finding out that Rhodochrosite helps to unite twin flames, I bought one, cleansed and charged it and told the crystal that I wanted it to bring my person to me. Less than 3 months afterwards, my twin flame and I became a couple.

2 Lucky Bamboos

You can tie 2 lucky bamboos of the same size with a red ribbon or red string and grow them together to attract your twin flame. You should see one of the plants as representing your person and the other as yourself. If the relationship corner of your home is cool and ventilated, you can place the pair in that area.

Remember to keep them in purified water and rounded stones/gravel, feed them when required and place a coin in the container with the plants. You can even place an insoluble crystal of your choice in the container also.

I used to have just one lucky bamboo growing all alone for over a year. Very soon after I tied another one to it, my twin flame and I started our relationship. Under the roots of both plants, I placed a raw Red Jasper so our relationship would remain healthy and passionate.

Twin Flame Rudraksha Seeds

Rudraksha seeds are very powerful and sacred items. They are believed to be blessed by many powerful gods and goddesses. These seeds have beneficial electromagnetic frequencies like crystals do. Like crystals, different types of Rudraksha seeds offer different benefits. The 2-faced seed and the Gauri Shankar seed will help you call in your twin flame easily and quickly.

Like crystals, Rudraksha seeds need to be cleansed and charged occasionally, and you can wear them, keep them close to you or place them in your home, office or car.

Pair of Mandarin Ducks

Having an image, carving or statue of a pair of mandarin ducks in your relationship corner will help you call in your twin flame. This practice has been done for thousands of years and has helped many people to unite with their twin flames.

Reiki

A 2nd degree Reiki practitioner or Master of the Usui Reiki system can use Reiki to help with any good purpose, including uniting twin flames. They can do this for themselves or for others.

You can request a session from a 2nd degree Reiki practitioner or a Reiki Master to help you unite with your twin flame. You would not need to be present for the session. Many Reiki practitioners charge for their sessions and this is good because both physical and spiritual workers deserve payment.

So, there you have it – the 7-step formula for quickly and easily attracting your twin flame. This is the formula I followed to attract my twin flame effortlessly and in a really short time.

I hope this book helps you feel more equipped, positive and confident, and that you use the given formula to call in your person easily and fast.

Enjoy the journey of uniting with your twin flame, growing together in happiness and helping others have happiness too.

Very best wishes to you and your twin flame,

Liliah

www.ingramcontent.com/pod-product-compliance
Lightning Source LLC
LaVergne TN
LVHW092204110225
803541LV00034B/331